Push and Pull Faces

by Allison K. Lim

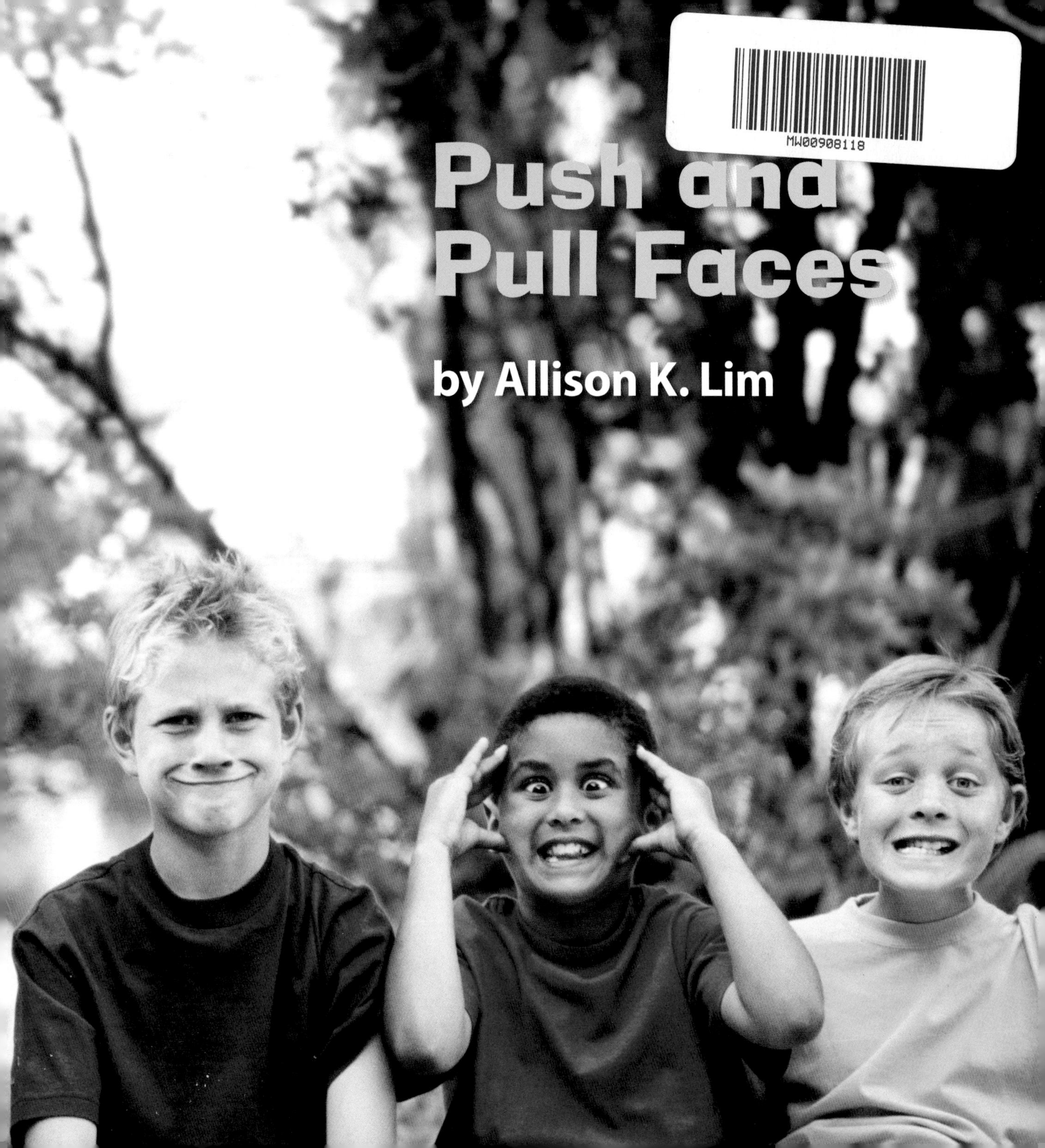

Push

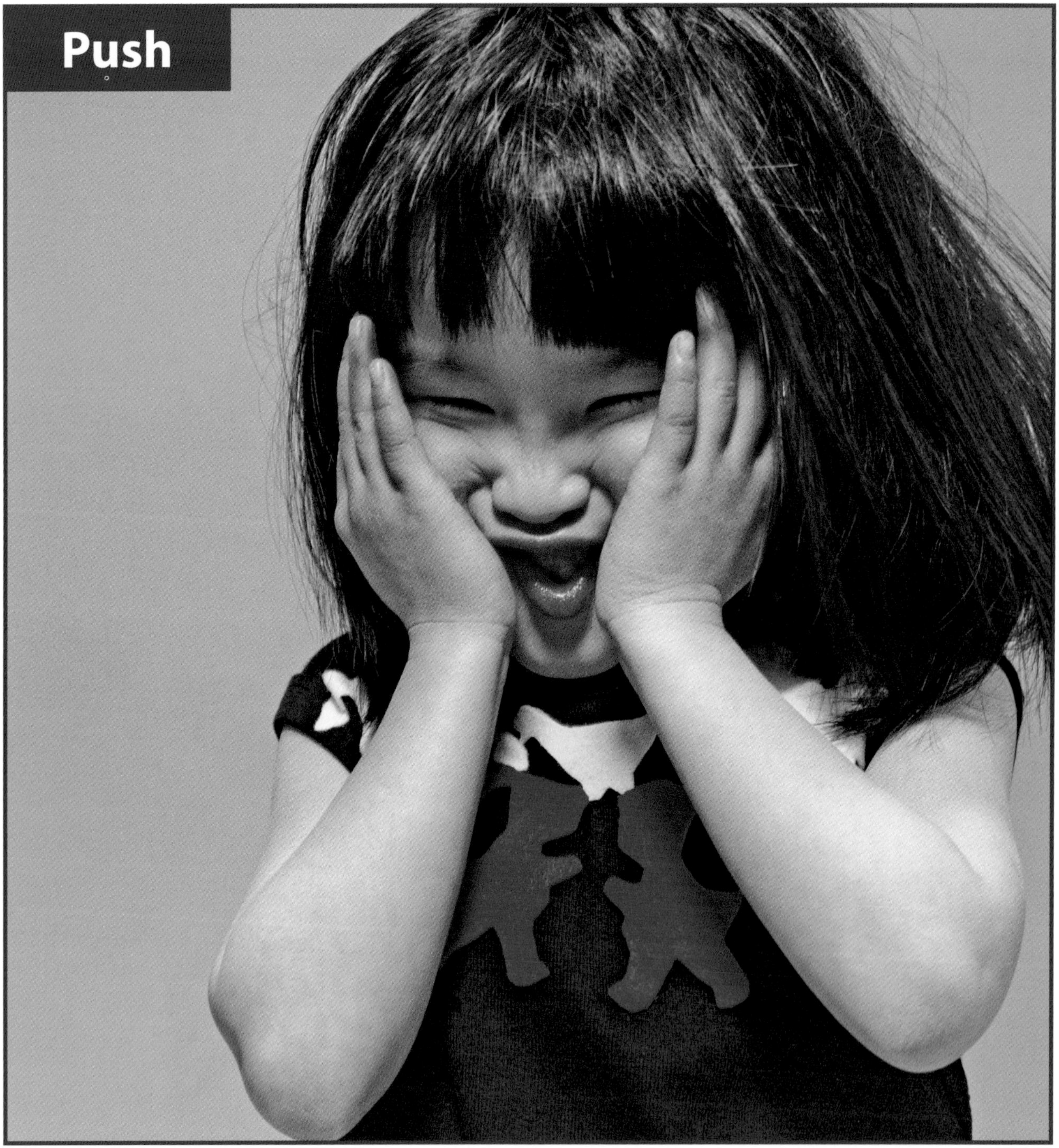

Pull

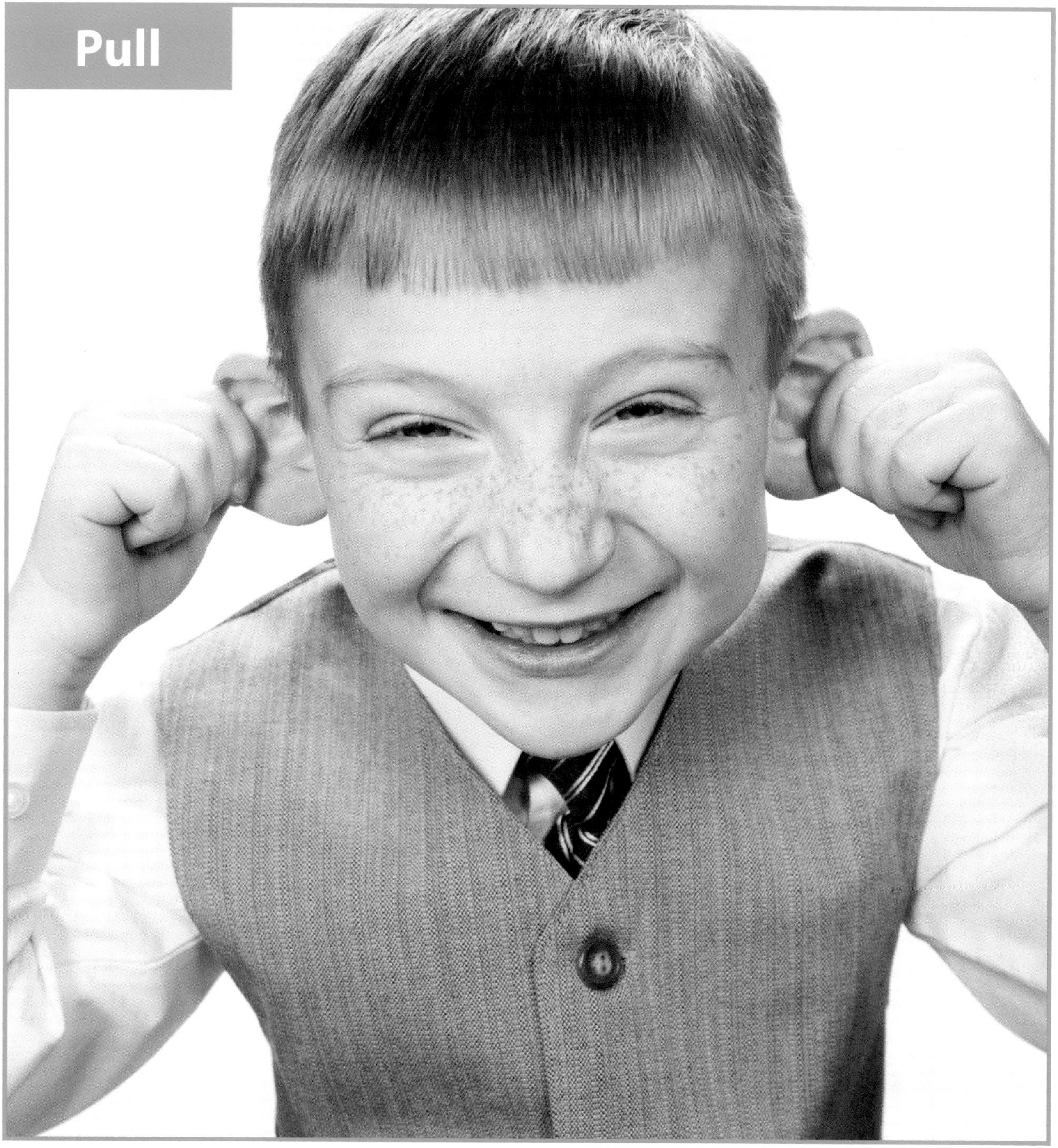

Push

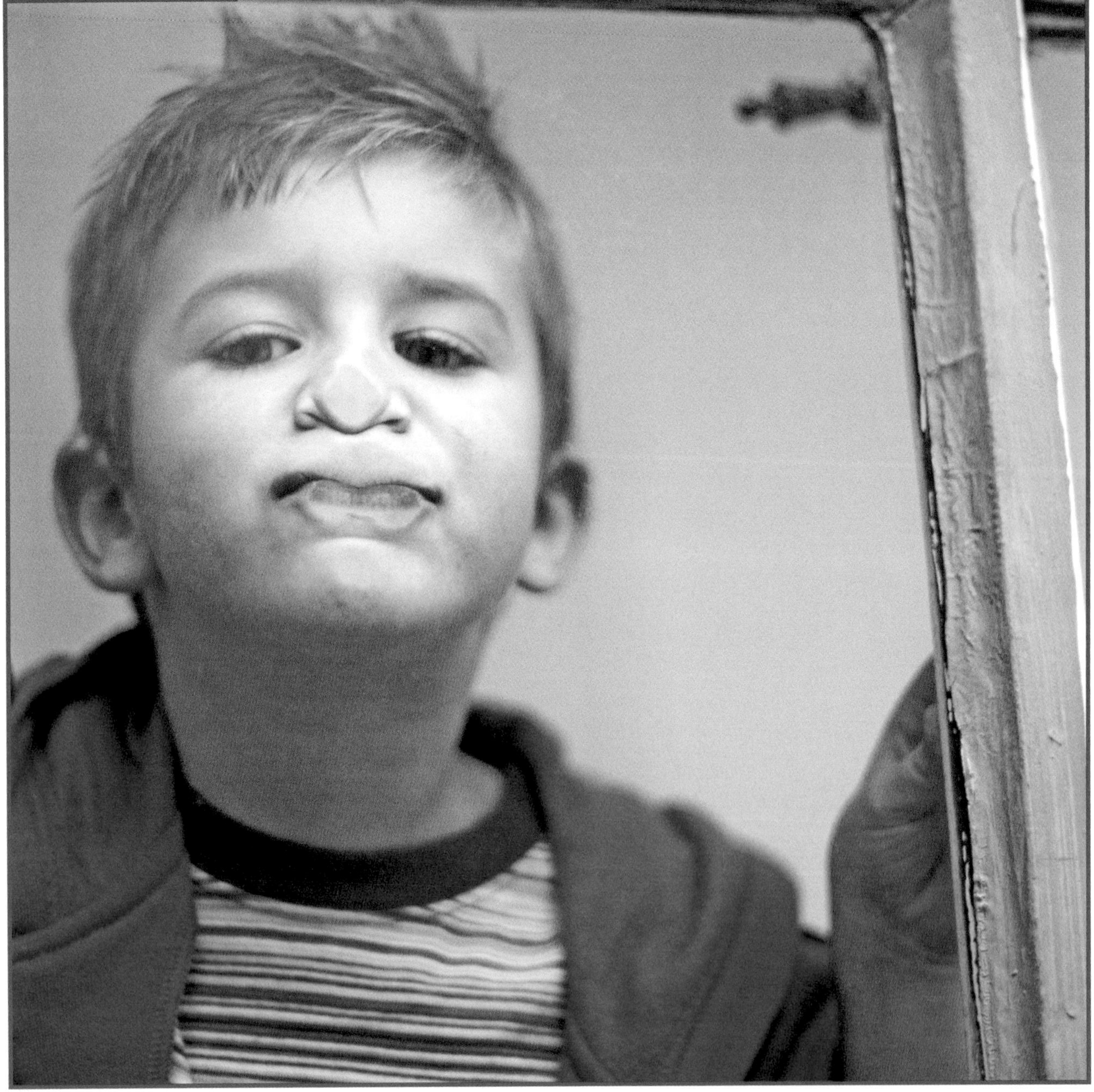

Pull

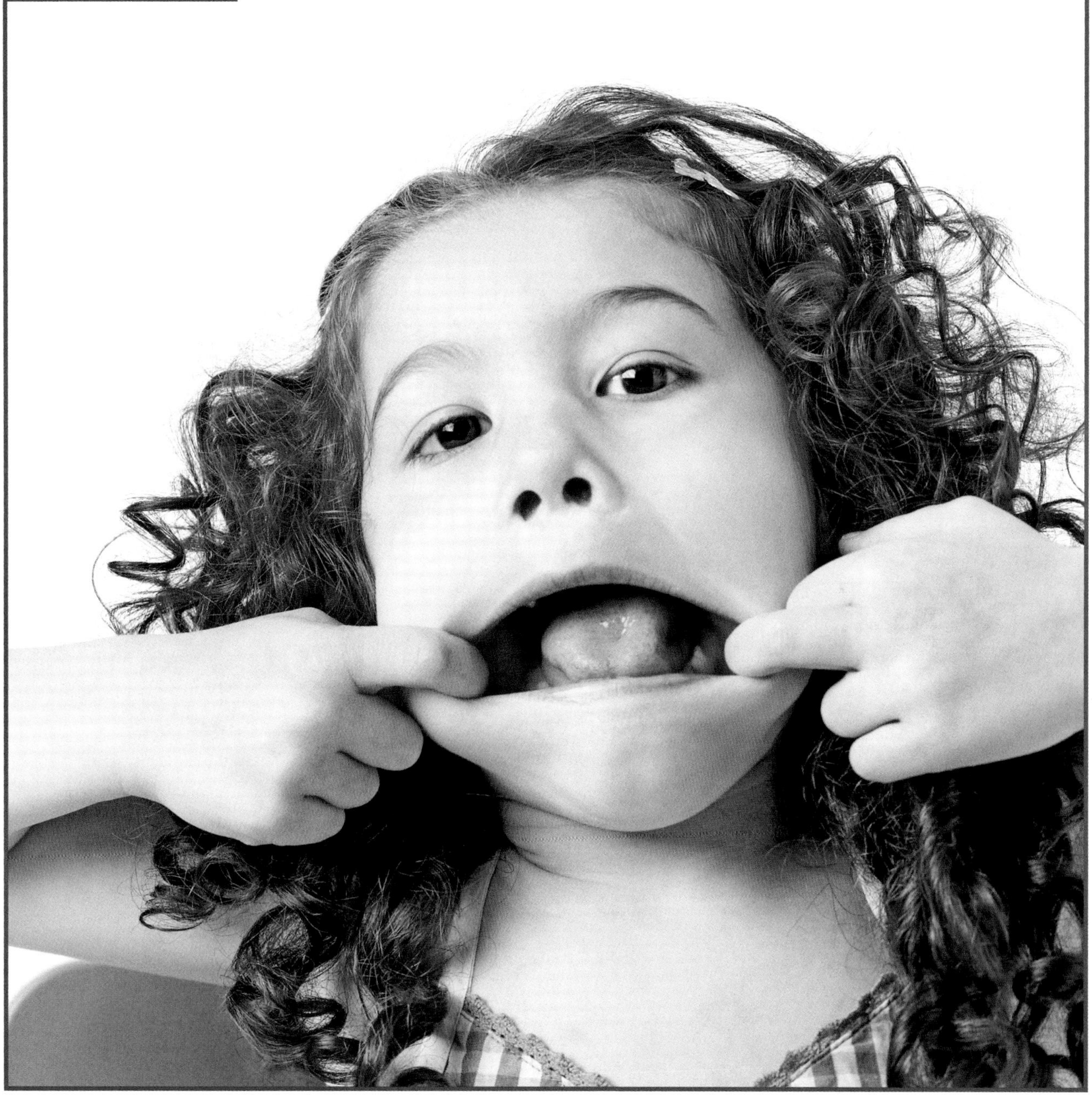

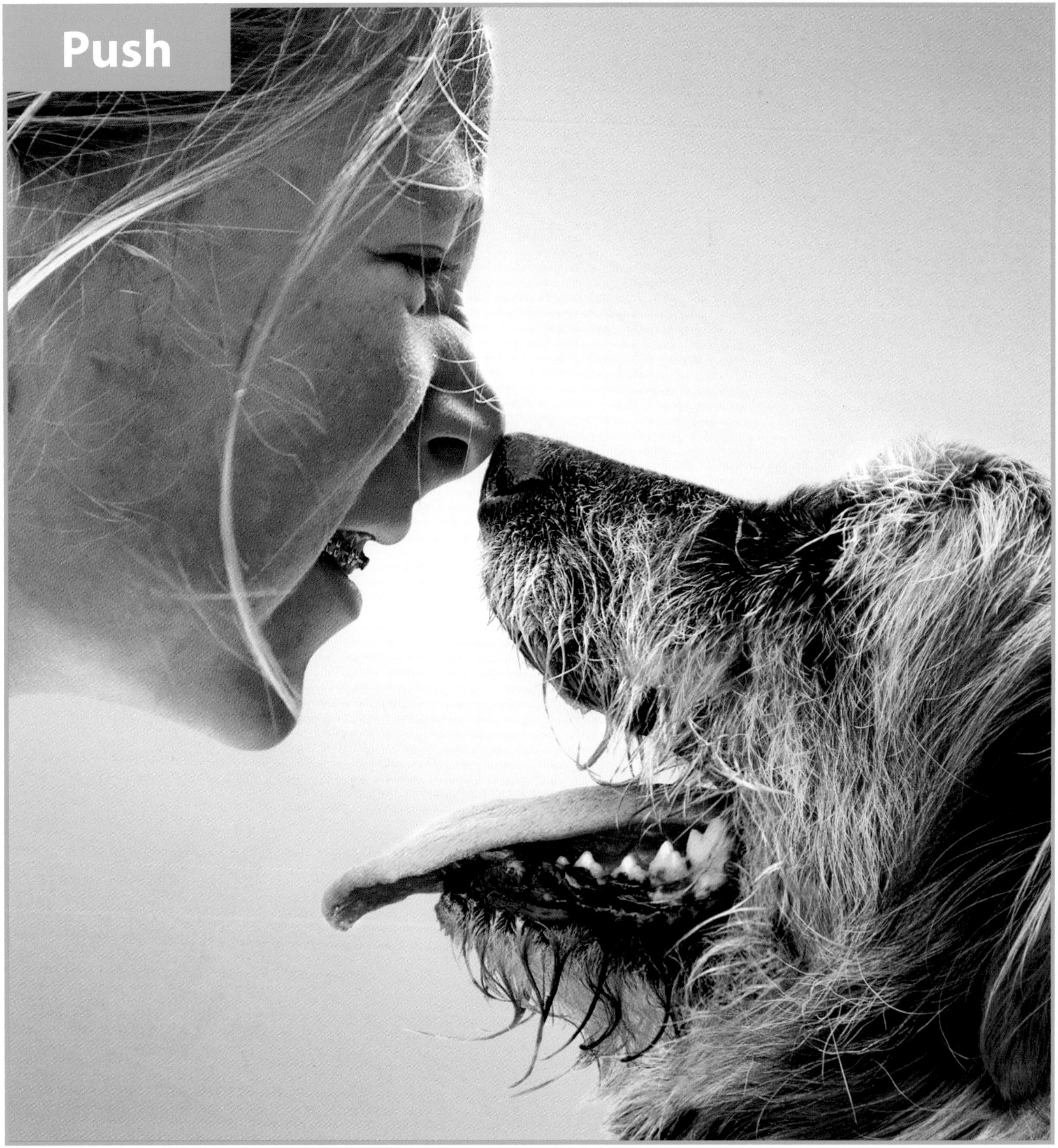
Push

Pull

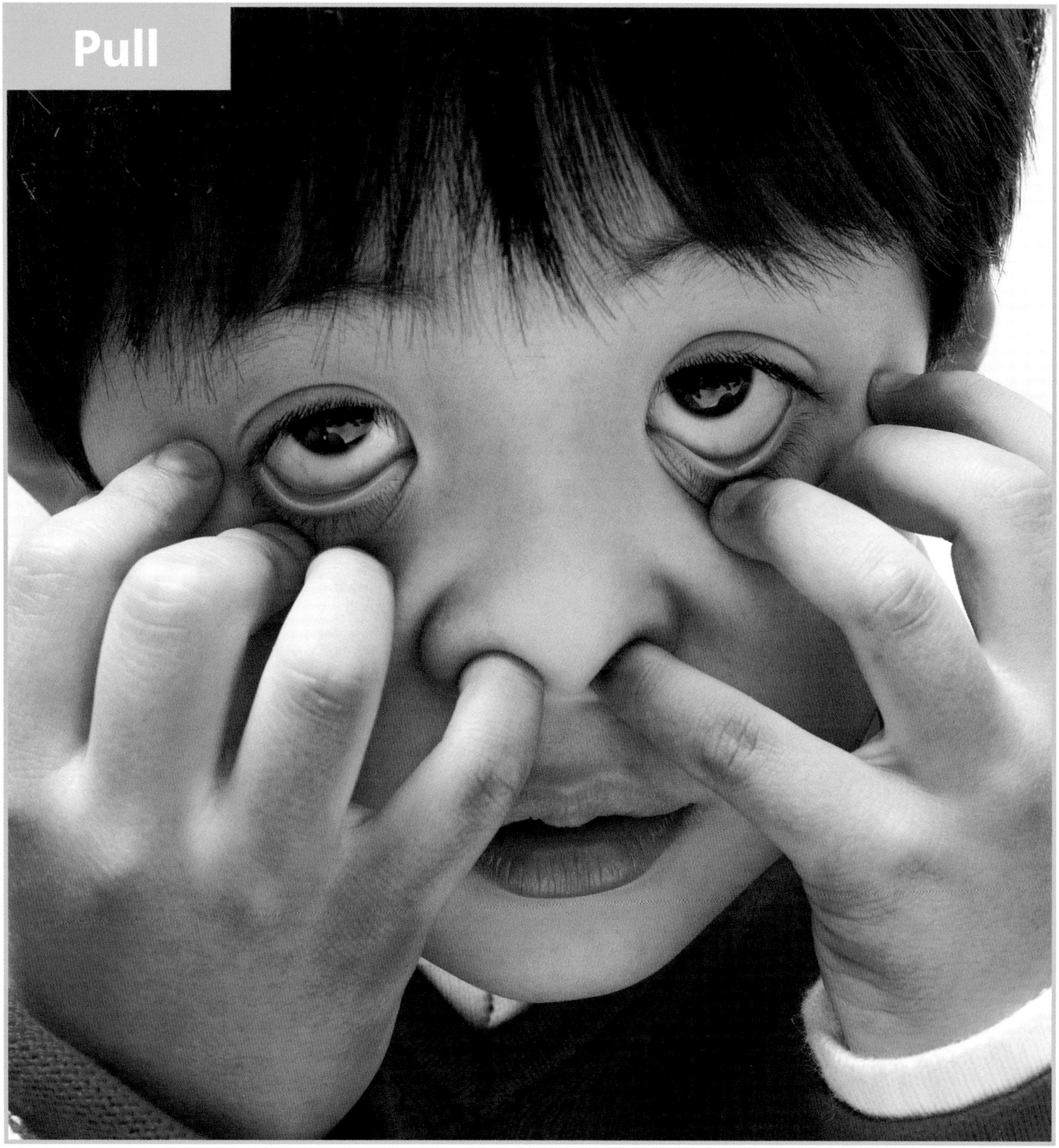

Push

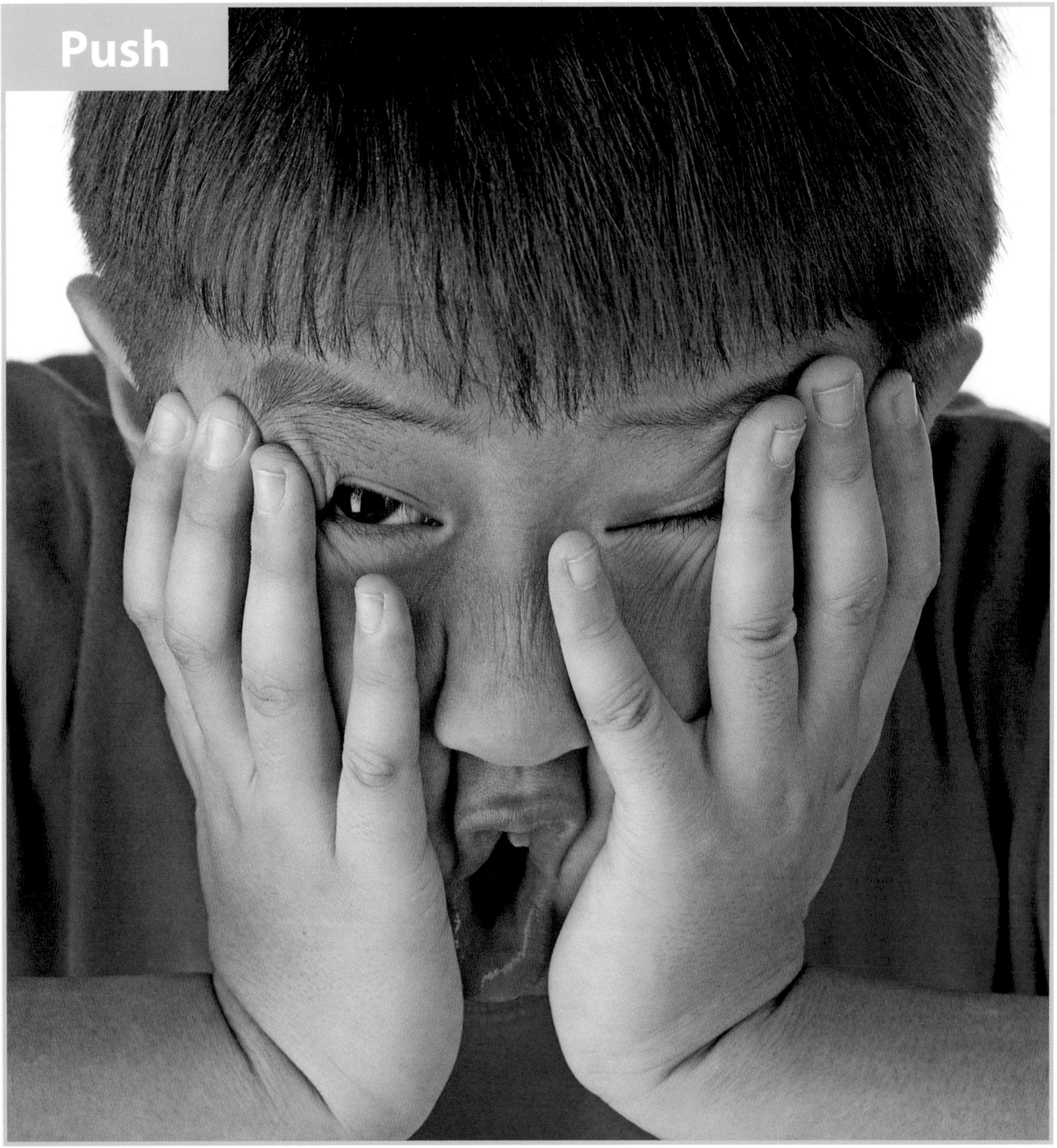

Pull

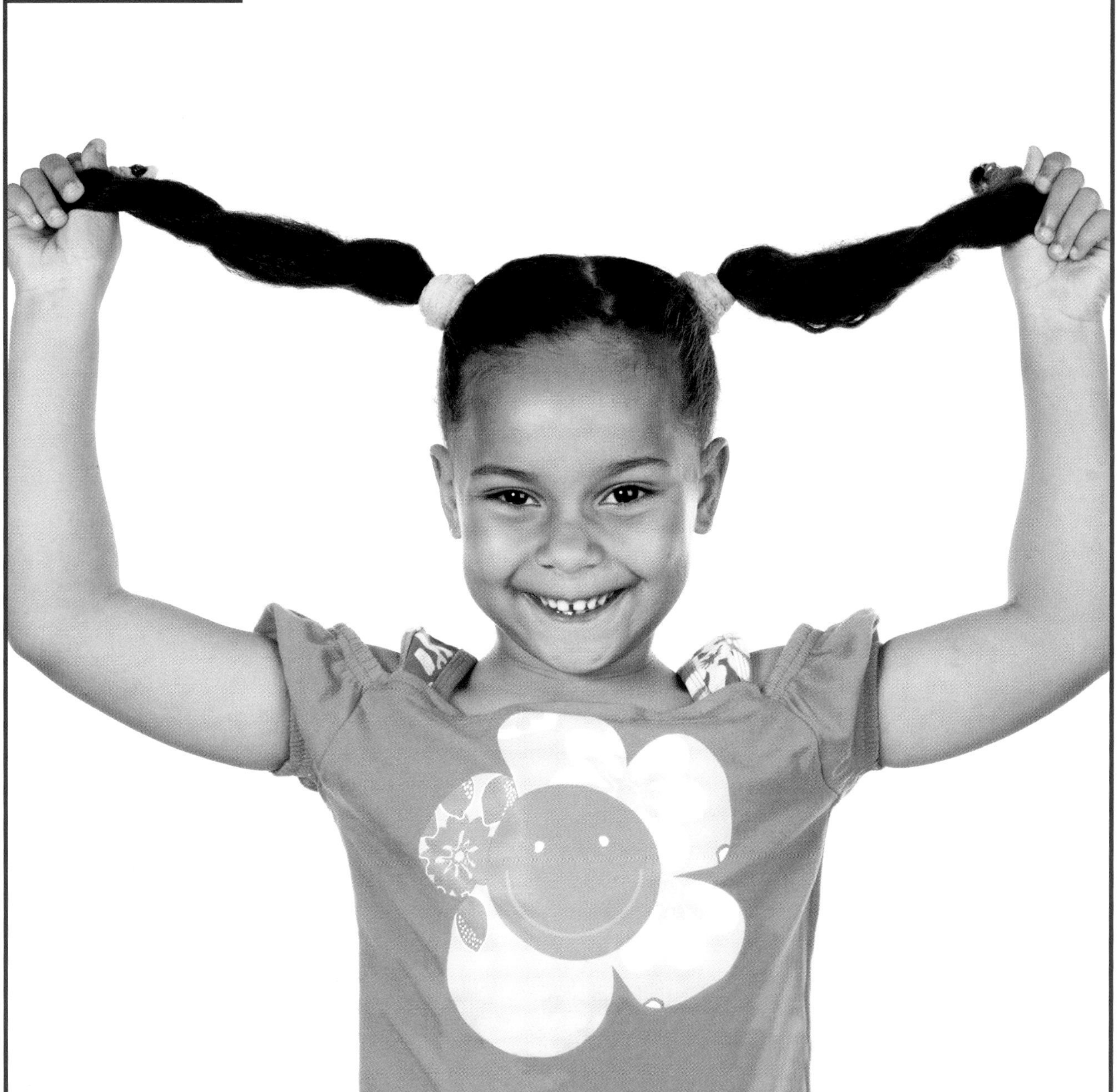

Push

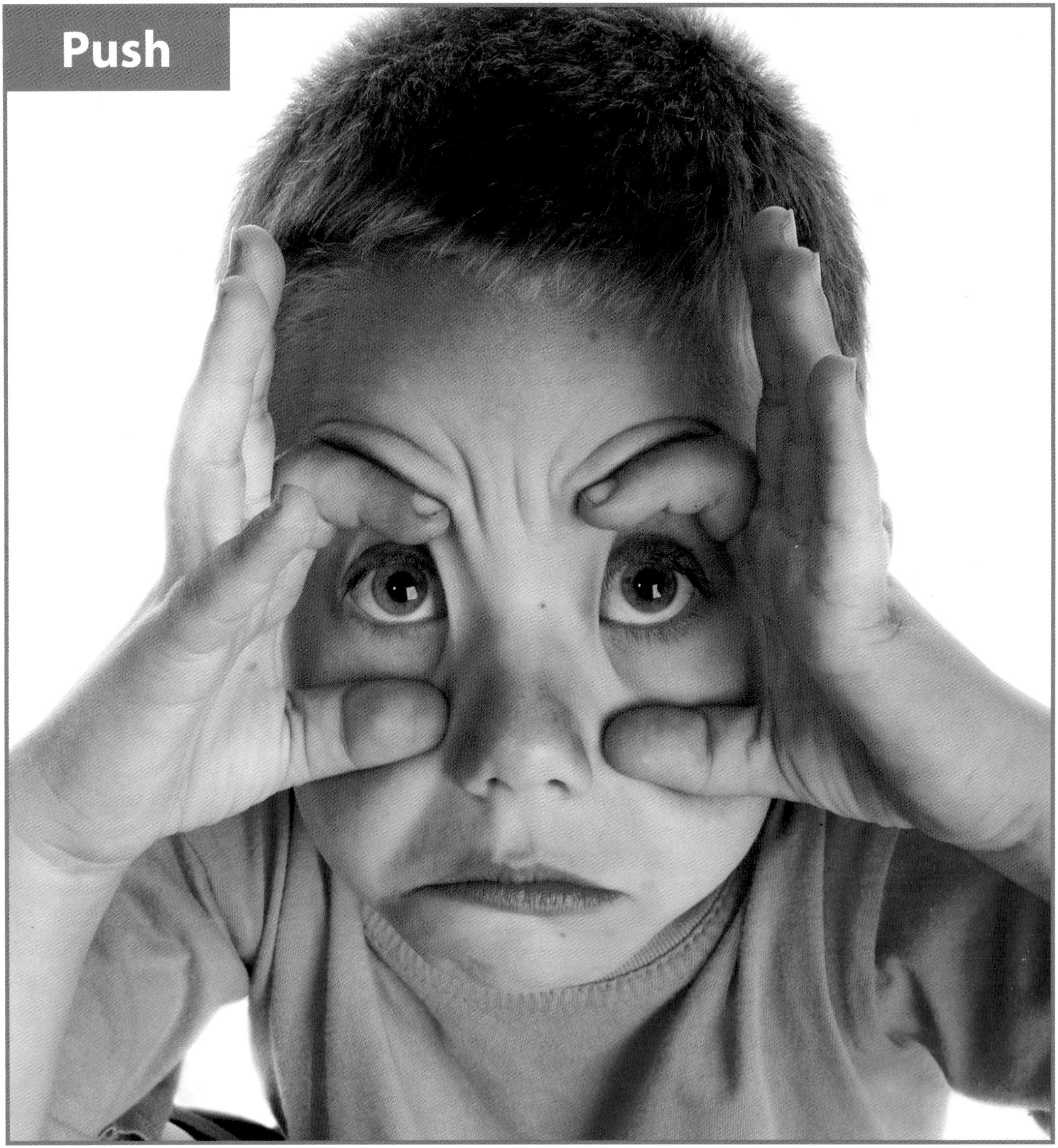

Pull

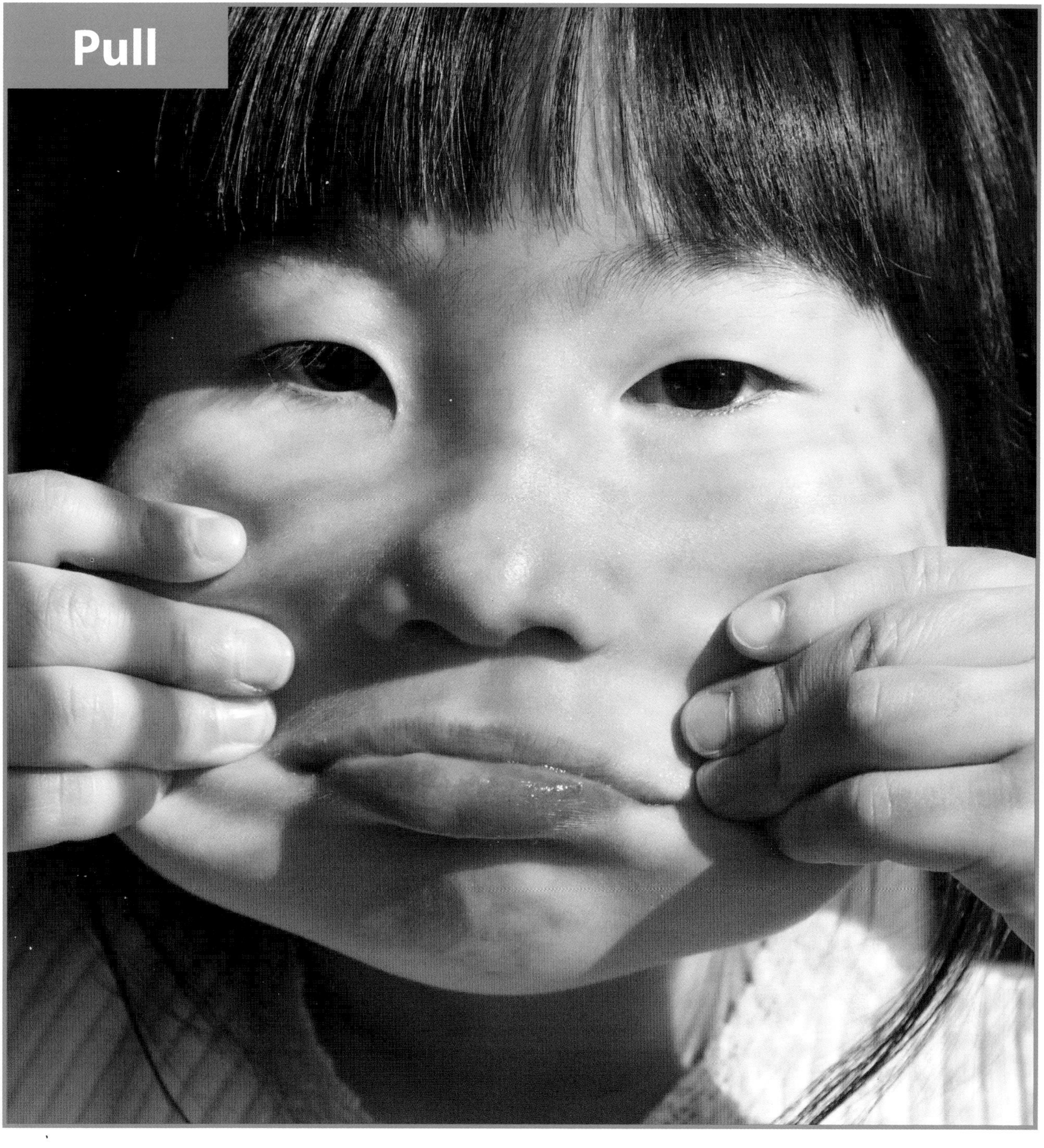

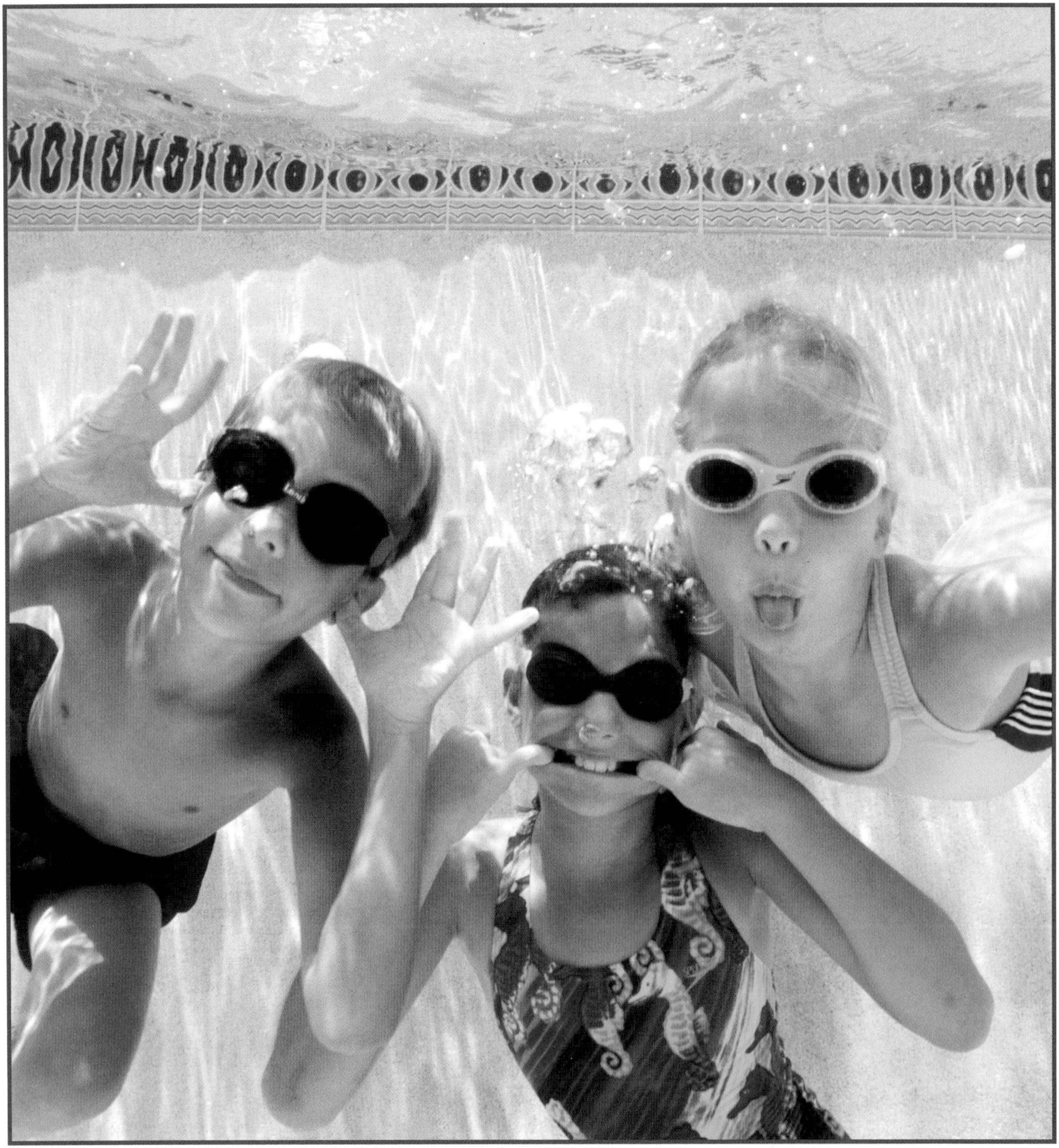